FOOTPRINTS OF
THE NORTHERN SAINTS

FOOTPRINTS OF THE NORTHERN SAINTS

✝

BASIL HUME

DARTON · LONGMAN + TODD

First published in 1996 by
Darton, Longman and Todd Ltd
1 Spencer Court
140–142 Wandsworth High Street
London SW18 4JJ

ISBN 0–232–52152–2

A catalogue record for this book is available from the British Library.

Acknowledgements
This book is based upon the television programme, *Return of the Saints*,
produced and directed by Joseph Fenton and Miles England, and written
by Basil Hume.

All photographs courtesy of the Leslie Garland Picture Library, Newcastle
upon Tyne; except pp. 12, 56 and 94, taken from the Maudelene
Television production, *Return of the Saints*. Map on p. 18 by Jeremy Dixon.

Scripture quotations are taken from the New Jerusalem
Bible, published and copyright © 1985 by Darton, Longman
and Todd Ltd and Doubleday & Co. Inc.

Phototypeset in 11/16½pt Caxton Book by Intype, London Ltd
Printed and bound in Great Britain
by BPC Wheatons Ltd, Exeter

CONTENTS

✠

illustrations

✠

What is life all about?

What are we here for?

Where is it all leading?

What happens after death?

These are questions which haunt people in our day. The early northern saints brought answers to these questions and those answers are as relevant today as they were in their time.

Basil Hume

Waves breaking against the rocks on the Northumbrian coast

PREFACE

✟

This is not a book by a professional historian. It is the work of an enthusiast for the north-east of England and for the saints of that area. I was pleased to be invited, and indeed privileged too, to take part in a television broadcast on Channel 4 entitled 'Return of the Saints'. The text of this book is in the main, though not entirely, from that broadcast.

This is no literary gem either. The spoken word looks clumsy, even crude, on the pages of a book. But I trust that what we have here will whet the reader's appetite to learn more about a subject and a period of history that is rich in interest and not, in my view, irrelevant in our day. Saints from all ages have something to say to us – their lives speak eloquently of God. We can be more touched by contact with holy people than by any number of sermons. At least I have found it to be so.

Another's strong faith and dedicated service of God at the same time rebukes us for our sluggishness and inspires us to change our ways. If God is so attractive to them, why should he not be so for us?

The aim of this book is, then, a limited one, but I like to think that if the text is inadequate – and it is – at least the pictures are beautiful. They, too, can inspire and their beauty will speak to us of God. I hope that this will be so.

Basil Hume with Bamburgh Castle behind him

✠

CHAPTER ONE

The Arrival of
the Saints

I invite you to return home with me, to north-east England, to walk in the footsteps of holy men and women who lived a long time ago, in the seventh and eighth centuries. I believe these holy men and women still have something important to say to us in our day. What always moves me when I read and think about the monk-bishops who introduced Christianity to Northumbria is that they were holy people, totally dedicated to the service of God and his people.

As a family we lived in the city, in Newcastle, but we would often visit parts of Northumbria on a day out, or we might go south of Newcastle to Durham where Saint Cuthbert is buried. On these trips I learned a little about the early northern saints, where they came from, where they lived, and something about the work they did. I feel that in some ways I have lived under their shadow all my life.

I want you to join me, and follow me, in this pilgrimage to meet these great personalities. They were not only very holy, but lived in a time of trouble, danger and conflict. In spite of the difficulties of their time, they managed to create what was in many ways a Golden Age within the Christian story of our land. I would like to think that you will share my enthusiasm for these people and this period in our history.

Picture if you can the royal castle of Bamburgh, and further in the distance Holy Island, which used to be called Lindisfarne, and nearby the Farne Islands. It is a beautiful part of our country. I can understand why the monks who came down from Iona settled on Holy Island. It is so beautiful; simply by being there, one's mind and heart inevitably seem to go up to God.

Lindisfarne was chosen for their home by the monks of Iona because twice a day it was cut off from the mainland by the tide. That gave the island some solitude. Nevertheless, it was close to, and under the shadow of, the local king. That relationship between the king and the monk-bishops was, as we shall see, very important in Anglo-Saxon Britain.

The missionaries who came with Saint Augustine could not have achieved what they did without the

Lindisfarne Priory ruins, Holy Island

support of the King of Kent, Ethelbert. Here in Lindis-farne, the close relationship between Saint Aidan and King Oswald was also of great significance for the Christianisation of Northumbria. After all, it was the kings who gave land upon which the monasteries were built and monasteries were the most powerful instru-ments of missionary activity in these islands.

On Holy Island, in Northumbria, the mission of the Celtic monks began. That beginning was largely due to King Oswald who, while exiled in Scotland, had been converted to Christianity. He knew the monks of Iona. He asked them to come and establish a monastery within his kingdom. It is this monastery, Lindisfarne, on Holy Island, which is the origin of Celtic Christianity in Britain.

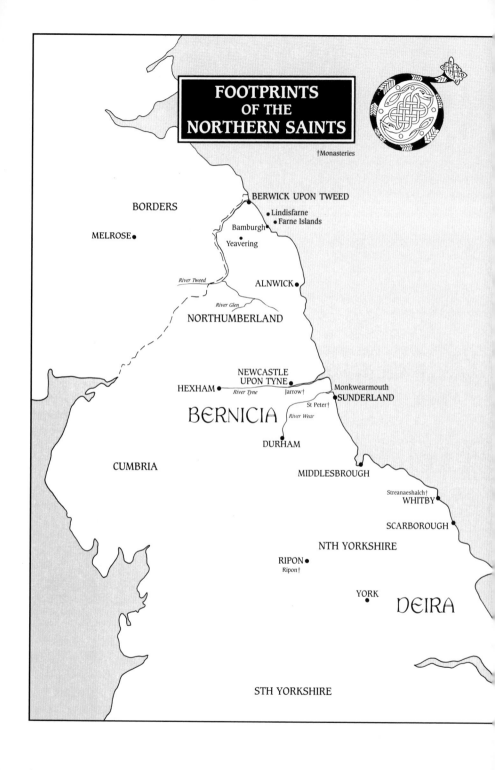

FOOTPRINTS OF THE NORTHERN SAINTS

†Monasteries

BORDERS

MELROSE●

BERWICK UPON TWEED
● Lindisfarne
● Farne Islands
Bamburgh●
Yeavering

River Tweed

ALNWICK ●

River Glen

NORTHUMBERLAND

NEWCASTLE
UPON TYNE ●
HEXHAM ●   *River Tyne*   Jarrow†
Monkwearmouth
St Peter† ●SUNDERLAND

BERNICIA   *River Wear*

DURHAM

CUMBRIA

MIDDLESBROUGH

Streanaeshalch†
WHITBY

SCARBOROUGH

NTH YORKSHIRE

RIPON ●
Ripon†

YORK
●

DEIRA

STH YORKSHIRE

✠

CHAPTER TWO

PAULINUS

In Anglo-Saxon England, the country was a mosaic of different kingdoms, often with great rivalry between them, often at war with one another. In Northumbria, for instance, there were two main sub-kingdoms, Bernicia and Deira, and they were often in conflict with one another, or together fighting other kingdoms.

The very first Christian missioner to arrive in the kingdom of Northumbria was Saint Paulinus, a monk of the Roman tradition. He came to King Edwin who had a camp at Yeavering.

Many years earlier, before he became pope, Gregory, as a monk in Rome, had been moved by the plight of young Britons being sold as slaves in the Roman markets. Determined to bring the Christian gospel to Britain, Pope Gregory appointed another monk, Saint

Augustine, to lead that mission. Arriving in Britain, Augustine presented himself to King Ethelbert of Kent. Ethelbert was not only a powerful ruler, but had married Bertha, a Frankish princess who was already a Christian. In a short time, Augustine had converted King Ethelbert. Christianity had been firmly planted on British soil, although only in Kent. Along with the other kingdoms, Northumbria remained to be converted.

Like Ethelbert in the south, Edwin had become a powerful ruler and had established Northumbria as a dominant kingdom. He had chosen a bride: she was Ethelburga, Ethelbert of Kent's daughter. She was a Christian, but he, Edwin, followed the religion of his Saxon ancestors. Edwin seemed sympathetic towards Christianity, and he allowed his bride to bring her chaplain, Saint Paulinus, along with her. Saint Paulinus was among the second group of monks sent by Pope Saint Gregory to help Saint Augustine. Paulinus had been preaching primarily in Kent and among the East Angles. In 625, he became a bishop and accompanied Ethelburga to Northumbria.

It took Paulinus four long years before he was able to begin his mission. His first opportunity arose at Easter in 628, when Edwin narrowly escaped an assassination attempt and, at the same time, witnessed the safe birth of his daughter, Eanfled. As was his custom, Edwin gave thanks to the gods. Paulinus, however, told him that it was Christ who was responsible for the safe birth of the child. Edwin gave Paulinus' claim some thought, and seeking advice from his council, became convinced by a story told by one of them.

A man's life on earth is short, the councillor explained, and we know nothing of what came before or what will come after. It is like a solitary sparrow flying through a banquet hall during winter. Inside, the hall is warm and comfortable, while outside winter storms rage. The sparrow flies into the hall from the stormy darkness and enjoys the comforting warmth. After a while, it flies out and returns to the darkness. Where the sparrow goes and where it came from we do not know. So it is with us. Edwin became convinced that any teaching which could penetrate the darkness should be followed, so he became a Christian. Once the king had been converted, Paulinus could begin, with the help of James the Deacon, to evangelise the kingdom of Northumbria.

Paulinus once spent thirty-six days instructing the people of Northumbria in the Christian faith and baptising in the River Glen. In so doing, he was carrying out the first responsibility of every bishop, and indeed of every priest, namely to preach the gospel of Christ and to administer the sacraments.

We hear so many stories of successful and dramatic conversions during this period of the Church's history.

Puffin with fish in its beak, Farne Islands

We are given the impression that great numbers of people became Christian through divine inspiration. We tend to forget, when hearing these stories, that divine inspiration was mediated through the tireless efforts and persistent commitment of men like Saint Paulinus who seized the historical circumstances of their time and place, persuasively using them in the service of the gospel.

We often hear that nobles and commoners became Christian for political reasons, to endear them to the reigning monarch or simply to go along with the crowd. That interpretation, however, fails to recognise the communal dimension of the life of the time. Religion was not considered only a matter of personal, one-on-one relationship with the divine. Rather, it was, as with so many other aspects of Northumbrian life, also a concern of the clan, of the people as a whole. That same communal dimension identified the king as reflecting and representing the whole of the clan. Edwin becoming a Christian was not only a personal, individual conversion, but the conversion of the whole people he led.

It was for this reason that Edwin consulted his advisers and seriously considered their recommendations. They were recommending a change not for Edwin alone, but for Edwin and the whole of the people. The story of the sparrow was convincing to

Edwin not simply for personal reasons but because it answered an important question for which the old religion of his people had no answer – what happens before and after life as we know it? A sensible, reasonable answer to this question would enrich the lives of all the people of Edwin's clan.

Paulinus had those answers and the personal conviction and ability to explain them in a manner that Edwin, as well as his people, could understand and appreciate. The communal dimension of Anglo-Saxon life would have had a direct connection with that of the Christian gospel and its message of love and caring for all men and women. It was, of course, also a facet of life with which Paulinus would have been accustomed, for the love of God and others is at the centre of the monastic life where prayer and work are pursued in common.

The common life, based on communion with God and our neighbour, could perhaps be identified as one of the principal thrusts of evangelisation today. People today are searching for the spiritual, and indeed also for community. They see in monasteries spiritual centres where God is at the heart of the life of the community. If people are in search of the spiritual, they will often find it by going to a monastery to see an individual monk, to take part in the communal prayer, or simply to absorb the atmosphere of the community, the centre of which is the praise and worship of God.

There are several important characteristics of a monastic community. The first is that each individual monk has to be seeking God. That is the one single, individual motive each monk needs to have. It has also, of course, to be part of the life of every Christian. Religion has to be of the mind and the heart, not something merely external. Men and women join monasteries because they experience a strong desire to spend their lives seeking God, guided by an abbot or abbess and in a community of persons with the same strong desire. The monk or nun has to love being involved in the praise and worship of God, the *Opus Dei*. The individual's search for God must lead to the communal praise of him.

The Rule of Saint Benedict demands a certain robustness and toughness to be able to keep going when life in the monastery is difficult, when faith seems weak or prayer is an experience of darkness. Such an approach is an important quality for our world today because so many people think that having a spiritual life means always being 'on a high'. In reality, for most people, a serious spiritual life involves going through darkness when faith is tried. Faith has to be purified in order for true charity to prevail.

The community aspect of monastic life is a living testimony to the importance of living generously for

God and others and in so doing to overcome any exaggerated individualistic self-interest.

Returning to Saint Paulinus, his work came to an abrupt end in 633 when Edwin was defeated and died during an invasion led by a Christian leader of the Welsh, allies of the anti-Christian King Penda of Mercia. Paulinus accompanied the queen and her children to Kent, under the protection of her brother King Eadbald. Edwin's territory was divided into the kingdoms of Deira and Bernicia. In 634, Oswald, who had an ancient claim to the throne of a united Northumbria, led a successful counter-invasion and became king.

Statue of Saint Aidan, Holy Island

CHAPTER THREE

✢

AIÐAN

King Oswald, as we mentioned earlier, turned to the monks of Iona for help in converting his new kingdom. The first monk they sent was unsuccessful. He found the Northumbrians too obstinate and barbarous. Thinking there was no future there, he returned to Iona.

The community of Iona was not satisfied with what he reported. A community meeting was held. Aidan rebuked the monk because he had tried to go too far too quickly with the Northumbrians, and this underlines what for me is a very important pastoral principle: pastors need to start where people are and not where they think they should be. They must then be gently led in a direction they would never have dreamed possible.

Aidan, to my way of thinking, was the perfect pastor. Even though he could not speak the language of the people of Northumbria, he found a way to preach. He went around with the king, and the king did the translating and interpreting for him.

There must have been something very compelling about Aidan. He was clearly a man of God and a man of prayer. That was the secret of his evangelising. When reading the lives of Aidan, Paulinus and other monk-bishops, it becomes more and more apparent that these men lived their faith. Their faith was so strong, so deep, that it flowed into their preaching and their actions. We often hear that the cathedrals of medieval England express the story of Christianity in their magnificent statuary and stained-glass windows. In their vaulted ceilings and soaring towers they move people towards God, towards something beyond the daily preoccupations of their lives in the world. The lives of Saints Paulinus and Aidan did the same. There was such a continuity between what they believed and what they preached, and between what they preached and what they lived, that people immediately saw and felt the living presence of God in their midst.

Aidan was a remarkable man. King Oswald was too. He recognised the truth as Aidan preached it. Perhaps even more remarkable was the relationship between the two. We might think they had very little in common. Oswald was a secular king whose attention was directed towards maintaining his kingdom, protecting

Lindisfarne Castle, Holy Island

his people, guarding them from the ever-present dangers of invasion, destruction and annihilation. Aidan's energy, on the other hand, was directed towards saving souls, towards helping people understand the great richness of life with God in their lives here on earth as well as in heaven.

The distinction between the temporal and the spiritual was not so marked in men like Oswald and Aidan as it is for people in our day. The relationship between monarch and monk-bishop also expressed a deep concern for the welfare of the people, their temporal as well as their spiritual well-being. Aidan, then, as a monk-bishop, and Oswald, a king, reflected real leadership, moving beyond their own respective areas of competence, to dedicate themselves to the people they led.

There is a story which expresses the depth of friendship and the quality of leadership shared by Aidan and Oswald. They were seated together at dinner when, as a silver dish filled with good things was placed before them, a steward announced that a large crowd was at the door begging for bread. Raising his right hand to signal a command, Oswald ordered that everything on the dish be given to them and that the dish itself be broken up into enough pieces for everyone. Saint Aidan, as the story is told, prayed that Oswald's right hand would never perish.

Unfortunately, in 642, eight years after the beginning of his reign, Oswald died at the hands of Penda, King of Mercia, who again invaded Northumbria. Penda divided Oswald's kingdom, and Oswin, Edwin's cousin, became King of Deira.

There is an interesting story about Saint Aidan and King Oswin. Oswin gave Aidan a horse because the king thought it would be more suitable for a bishop to ride a horse than to travel on foot. One day Aidan met a beggar, and having nothing to give except the horse, he gave the horse away. The king was not very pleased about this and rebuked Aidan. But Aidan was not to be swayed from the conviction of his faith. In a rather stern and direct manner, he responded to the king, 'Which is more important, this child of a mare or this child of God?' The king was covered in confusion, and it is said that he went down on his knees and asked Aidan forgiveness for his pride.

This story says much about Saint Aidan, about the way he lived his faith, and about the simplicity of that faith. We might ask whether Aidan could have had such a profound influence over Oswin had he not lived what he believed, had he not reflected the living presence of God in the totality of his life.

All of us today are challenged by Aidan's authenticity and simplicity. Such simplicity of life has two levels: the first is single-mindedness, being so concentrated on God and serving him that other things are subordinate to that; the second level is simplicity of life-style, trying to live lives of material simplicity. This is what speaks to people outside the Church. As Paul VI says, 'Modern man listens more readily to witnesses than to teachers; if they listen to teachers it is because they are witnesses.'

Aidan died in 651, near Bamburgh, having spent sixteen years working for the conversion of Northumbria to Christianity. When Aidan first arrived in Northumbria, little remained of Paulinus' endeavours. However, during the years of Aidan's mission, Lindisfarne was firmly established as a monastery from which monks were sent out to convert the Anglo-Saxons to Christianity. Lindisfarne became, then, not only a centre for its community of monks, but also a centre for the spiritual life of Northumbria.

Whitby Abbey ruins

✝

the synod of whitby

Aidan was succeeded by Finan and he, in turn, by Colman as Abbot of Lindisfarne. Finan's great achievements were the conversions of Peada, the son of the aggressively anti-Christian Penda, and also of the Mercians he ruled. At Finan's death, in 661, Colman became the third Abbot and Bishop of Lindisfarne. As with Aidan and Finan before him, Colman was born in Ireland and was sent to Lindisfarne from Iona.

It was during Colman's time as Abbot of Lindisfarne that a major controversy in the early history of English Christianity was resolved at the Synod of Whitby in 664. The controversy was inevitable because the early missioners to England, although all monks, originated in two distinctly different places and brought with them their own respective customs and traditions.

In the south, the mission begun by Saint Augustine reflected a Roman monastic tradition. After all, he had been sent to England by Pope Saint Gregory the Great, himself a Roman and a monk. In the north, Aidan had brought the Celtic tradition from Iona which had its roots in the Irish Church. Historically, Christianity in Ireland had moved in a direction which differed from the way things were done in Rome. So there were differences, and as the two traditions were followed side-by-side in the same land, there came a point when the differences had to be resolved. One such difference was the date for Easter.

Oswy had become king of a united Northumbria when, in 651, as king of Bernicia, he conquered Deira and had Oswin put to death. It was Oswy who called the Synod of Whitby. He wanted to resolve the conflicts between the Celtic and Roman traditions within his own kingdom. These differences had practical as well as political implications. On one and the same day, King Oswy and Bishop Colman celebrated Easter while the queen and her chaplain from Kent celebrated Palm Sunday. The two Northumbrian sub-kingdoms also reflected this division as Bernicia followed the Celtic tradition and Deira the Roman one. As in today's liturgical calendar, the designation of the date for the celebration of Easter was important in Anglo-Saxon times as well. It was the pivotal feast around which the dates of other feasts, and of the entire Church year, were determined.

Among the principal participants at the conference were Oswy who followed the Celtic tradition and his son Alfrid who championed the Roman one. Abbot Colman of Lindisfarne argued for the Celtic tradition, while advocating the Roman tradition was the Abbot of Ripon, Wilfrid, who, though only about thirty years old, had become known for his learning of and commitment to the Roman tradition. In fact, the community at Ripon had been established by Alfrid who himself named Wilfrid, once a monk at Lindisfarne, as abbot.

The problem was basically a result of history and chronology. The Celtic tradition continued to follow those practices of the Roman Church which had been established at the time of Saint Patrick. These had been preserved by Saint Columba and his successors at Iona and other Celtic monasteries. Shortly before Augustine arrived in Kent, the Roman Church had decreed changes which Augustine and his followers had implemented in their missions. Aidan and his followers, however, had adhered to the older practices of the Celtic monasteries.

Another difference had to do with the monastic practice of tonsure. Far more significant, however, were questions of authority and the universality of the Church. In effect, the controversies surrounding the

Synod of Whitby reflected the wider concerns of the Christian Church as it continued to define itself and create a greater consistency between its theology and its practice. Throughout the known world of the time, the rapidly spreading Christian faith had created its own local customs and traditions. The differences, as we observed earlier, had caused practical as well as theoretical problems.

These problems were of greater importance in Anglo-Saxon England than they would seem to be for us today. They touched the very heart of life, with all kinds of implications in civil and ecclesial matters, in ordinary, everyday living, since the society of that time did not distinguish between Church and state, religion and politics, as we do so readily today. Those kinds of distinction were, indeed, unknown and inconceivable; what we regard as two separate spheres of life were interwoven into a singularity of thought and practice, both for Anglo-Saxon England in general and Northumbria in particular.

For Oswy it was a question of uniformity of practice within his own kingdom at a time when something as apparently insignificant as the date for celebrating Easter threatened the internal unity of the kingdom.

Abbot Colman of Lindisfarne based his argument for following the Celtic tradition on loyalty and devotion to Saint Patrick and, more directly, to Saint Columba.

Abbot Wilfrid, on the other hand, argued for the Roman tradition and loyalty to the pope.

The issue of recognising the authority of Rome and the successors of Saint Peter came down to this question that King Oswy asked Wilfrid and Colman: 'Is it true that special authority was given to Saint Peter?' Colman answered, 'It is true, your majesty.' Then the king continued, 'Do you both agree that these words were indisputably addressed to Peter in the first place, and that our Lord gave him the keys of the kingdom of heaven?' Both answered that they did. At this, the king concluded, 'I tell you Peter is guardian of the gates of heaven, and I shall not contradict him. I shall obey his commands and everything to the best of my knowledge and ability. Otherwise, when I come to the gates of heaven, there may be no one to open them because he who holds the key was turned away.'

Thus the questions and controversies were settled by King Oswy. To many people today this may all seem rather remote and not very important, but there was a deeper issue that lay behind these discussions of the date of Easter. It was this: was the Christian Church in this island going to be separate from the universal Church and develop along its own lines, or was it going to be part of the universal Church, accepting the authority of the successor of Saint Peter?

This is very important for us today. The Church must

have authority, for whatever people may say we cannot live without it. We need to be in communion with Saint Peter and the local churches need to be in communion with each other. It is only through Peter, the guardian of the gates of heaven, that we can have a guarantee and protection of the faith which we have.

One of the problems in religion arises from the obvious fact that we cannot touch God, we cannot hear his voice, we cannot see him, which means there is great scope for an 'anything goes' mentality. It is, therefore, very important for the Church that Peter has special authority to teach and to act as a guarantor of the faith.

The Synod of Whitby and King Oswy's allegiance to the authority of Saint Peter united all of Christian England in one tradition and practice of the faith, and also united England with the greater universal tradition of the Roman Church. Presiding over the Abbey of Whitby, and a member of the Synod, was another remarkable person in Anglo-Saxon England, Saint Hilda.

Whitby Abbey interior

CHAPTER FIVE

✝

ḢILÐA

Saint Hilda was a descendant of King Edwin of Northumbria, the influential ruler of Paulinus' time,
and also the spiritual protégé of Saint Aidan who moni-
tored her spiritual development. Indeed her monastery
followed the Celtic tradition.

Hilda had been Abbess of Hartlepool, but in 657 she
founded the double monastery of Streanaeshalch, later
called Whitby by the Danes. It was not by accident that
Hilda's Abbey of Whitby was chosen as the site of
the Synod. It had become one of the greatest, if not *the*
greatest, centre of learning in north-east England. That
designation can, of course, be attributed to Saint
Hilda's leadership.

Whitby was a double monastery, one of several at
the time, where men and women constituted a single
community. They lived separately but came together in

the same abbey church for prayer. To Hilda's charismatic leadership is attributed the reputation of Whitby where, rather than being a cause for disagreeable scandals, both the men and the women of the community were considered exemplary in holiness and learning.

In addition to prayer, the monasteries of Anglo-Saxon England encouraged learning. In Hilda's Abbey of Whitby women as well as men studied the scriptures. Each monastery had its own school and established learning as an important dimension of its mission, indeed of its very existence. As the Roman tradition became more and more established, the significance of the Latin language grew, and the religious men and women of the Anglo-Saxon monasteries joined the universal Church in promoting Roman culture and knowledge. In addition to the scriptures, the men and women of the monasteries read the early writings of the Church in both Latin and Greek.

It is because of the monasteries that the English language we so cherish today was developed and preserved. Rather than promoting Latin as the exclusive language of learning and literacy, the monasteries also encouraged the native language of the Anglo-Saxons, especially its poetry.

Hilda must have had an especially influential role in recognising the significance of the Anglo-Saxon language, for the story of her discovery of Caedmon has been recorded. Caedmon was a poor, elderly cowherd who could neither read, write nor sing. In fact, he was so ashamed of his inability to sing that, in the company of others, as the harp was passed from one person to another for additional verses of a poetic ode, he would leave the group and return to his cows.

One night, as the story is told, a visitor entered his dreams, told him to sing, and, ignoring his reluctance, encouraged him to sing of the creation of the world. As Caedmon began to sing, the farmer who employed him heard it and took him to see Abbess Hilda. She brought him into the company of her greatest scholars who instructed him in some of the passages of the scriptures with which he was unfamiliar, and commissioned him to set them to music. The next day he returned with a superlative song and Hilda immediately encouraged him to join her men's monastery and pursue his gifted talent. Caedmon accepted Hilda's invitation and entered the monastery. There, he listened as the monastic scholars recounted scriptural passages to him, then he transposed them to music and poetry.

This story reflects Saint Aidan's influence on Saint Hilda. Aidan evangelised the people of Northumbria by leading them into the gospel message with simple, basic stories and truths which they could easily and immediately grasp, rather than by beginning with more sophisticated and difficult aspects of the mysteries of

Christianity. In doing this, it is clear that Aidan was concerned not to reject the people and their deeply felt customs and culture, nor to judge them as ignorant, obtuse or barbaric.

Hilda, likewise, saw great potential in Caedmon even though his humble work and inability to sing would have led others to dismiss him immediately. She recognised his God-given talent and provided him with a place in which that talent could flourish.

Hilda was well known as an adviser on spiritual matters. People came from all over the land to seek her counsel. She was also a preacher of some distinction and a born ruler. No doubt her background as a royal princess would have prepared her for that role, as well as the guidance of Aidan. Hilda is an example of the riches that women can bring to the Church in our day as spiritual advisers, teachers and leaders.

It is precisely as leaders that Hilda and other holy men and women of her day left us such a rich legacy of learning and education. As the barbaric Franks and Lombards, respectively in present-day France and Italy, continued to pillage and destroy, the situation there made learning and preservation of our valuable cultural heritage almost impossible. It was in the monasteries of England where that culture and heritage were preserved, not only for us, but for the entire Western world.

The significance of the monasteries as great centres of learning, of cultural preservation and of faith cannot be underestimated, even for our day. It was the monasteries and their schools which encouraged the commoners and kings of Anglo-Saxon England to equate nobility of life with nobility of learning and intellectual pursuits. Moreover, the fact that the monasteries encouraged literacy in the native language of the Anglo-Saxons as well as the imported language of Latin reflects an appreciation for language and communication on every level of human life. Implicit in the language of a people, and intricately tied to it, is a relationship between their very identity and their dignity. It is to the great credit of Hilda and the Anglo-Saxon monastic tradition that this relationship was recognised and appreciated. The appreciation of the language of the people of Anglo-Saxon England, and its higher forms of prose and poetry, is a direct expression of the monastic appreciation of the esteem and dignity of the people themselves as created by God. It is perhaps also an expression of the kind of unconditional love of the gospel message. It would have been so easy to categorise these people as barbaric and incapable of grasping the richness of the Christian faith, to deride their culture and language, and to dismiss them as unworthy. Instead, Saint Hilda, the other abbots and abbesses, the monk-bishops, of

Anglo-Saxon England created the monasteries as centres not only of learning and of the faith, but of a central truth of that faith which can so easily be taken for granted today: the unconditional love of God for all men and women, regardless of social status or of cultural and ethnic origin.

Embleton Bay

✝

CHAPTER SIX

ChEODORE OF CARSUS

Once the Synod of Whitby had united the whole of England to the Roman tradition, implications of that decision, beyond the consistent dating of Easter, became evident. The very structure and organisation of the Church became an acknowledged concern.

The Celtic tradition focused on the monastery as the seat of authority, and on the abbot as the central authoritative figure. Although most of them had been ordained bishops, it was by virtue of their role as abbot that they exercised authority. Some monks, who were not abbots, had been appointed bishops, but their authority was subject to that of the abbot.

The role of the bishop was more functional than juridical. That function was, indeed, of great significance, for the bishop was charged with administering certain sacraments which went beyond the role of priest or deacon. The role of the priest was that of evangelising, bringing people into Christian belief and practice, and afterwards of nurturing and supporting their new faith by providing for Eucharistic celebrations, Reconciliation, and Anointing the Sick. At the same time, the priest would be in direct contact with the people, continuing to strengthen and foster their growth and development in the new faith.

The bishop, on the other hand, would formally receive new and adult Christians into the Church, by administering the sacrament of Confirmation. He could also ordain new priests and deacons, although the tendency was to have the abbot-bishop do so. Clearly, then, the monastery itself was a centre of Christian life in Anglo-Saxon England in ways which went beyond its important cultural, social and spiritual role.

It was the place where the abbot presided and led the monks and the nuns who, in turn, evangelised and nourished the people in their newly discovered faith. This hierarchical structure and distribution of functions, with its explicit distinction of roles and accompanying social status, is essentially that followed today in the Church as well as in other organisations. Theologically and spiritually, these distinctions are not based as strongly on heredity as they were in the early medieval world, but rather on an acceptance and appreciation of differing gifts and talents, and the best use of those talents for service to the organisation as a whole.

There is, however, a major difference in the ecclesiastical order of the Celtic tradition we have been discussing and that to which we have become accustomed. It is basically a reversal of the roles of abbots and bishops. In the Roman tradition, both theologically and practically, it is the bishop rather than the abbot whose authority is primary. This was the practice of the Roman tradition established by Augustine in Canterbury, Kent, and throughout southern England. The Synod of Whitby signalled a change in Northumbria as well.

To bring this change into reality, and to unite all of England with the Roman tradition, Theodore of Tarsus was sent from Rome as Archbishop of Canterbury in the year 669, shortly after the Synod of Whitby. He accomplished a basic reorganisation of the Church into dioceses, creating many new ones, and established Canterbury as the Primatial See, that is, as the centre of ecclesiastical authority for all of England. The bishops were given authority, even over abbots, according to the Roman tradition. Of course, this was not accomplished overnight, and several of the abbots maintained their dual titles. Their authoritative designations were, however, transferred from their roles as abbots to their roles as bishops.

Basil Hume sailing amongst the Farne Islands

Theodore had been born in Tarsus, the home of Saint Paul, and died in Canterbury in 690, twenty-one years after he arrived there. So great was his influence that he is often referred to as a second founder of the Church in England.

What, then, is the true role of a bishop? There are three principles which have been very important for me. The first one relates to Christ's attitude to the marginalised. We see this in the calling of Matthew, the tax collector. Such persons were held in very low esteem for they were considered to be dishonest, apart from working for the Roman occupiers of their land.

As Jesus was walking on from there he saw a man named Matthew sitting at the tax office, and he said to him, 'Follow me.' And he got up and followed him. (Matthew 9:9)

Jesus welcomed the outcasts, the weak, those society does not value:

The tax collectors and sinners, however, were all crowding round to listen to him, and the Pharisees and scribes complained saying, 'This man welcomes sinners and eats with them.' (Luke 15:1–2)

The second principle for me as a pastor comes from the parable of the wheat and the tares in which Jesus warns that if you pull up the tares you may also tear up the wheat, and so ruin the crop (Matthew 13:24–30). This is a very delicate pastoral principle and means that sometimes we need to let things that are wrong continue for the time being lest in trying to put them right we make things worse. Adopting this principle will mean that we shall receive a lot of criticism. People tend to want bishops to condemn when they think they spot error or hear a dissenting voice.

My third principle comes from the Rule of Saint Benedict: 'Let the abbot always set mercy before justice, that he himself may obtain mercy. Let him hate evil, but love the brethren. In administering correction let him act prudently and not go to excess, lest being too zealous in removing the rust he break the vessel. Let him always distrust his own frailty and remember that the bruised reed is not to be broken. By this we do not mean that he should allow evils to grow but that, as we have said above, he should eradicate them prudently and with charity in the way that may be seen best in each case . . . Let him so temper all things that the strong may still have something to long after, and the weak may not draw back in alarm.' (Rule of Saint Benedict, ch. 64)

When considering a person's suitability to become a bishop, I would tend to look for someone who is, first and foremost, a good human being and he must have a sense of humour. I would also want a bishop to be naturally kind. Of course it is always difficult to be kind with people who annoy you or phone you in the middle of the night, but kindness is an important quality. We do most harm as bishops and priests when we are unkind. Kindness and compassion go together. I would look for selflessness, probably the hardest area. It is the one which troubles my own conscience most, for I know my failures in this aspect of my life.

I doubt whether many bishops think that they are equal to the task. I have a feeling that if they think they are, then they should not be bishops. I spend quite a lot of my life worrying because I am neglecting some part of my ministry. It is impossible to do adequately all that we are called to do, and I suspect that most bishops find that. A bishop's main responsibility is the care of priests and people. In a very large or busy diocese, it is difficult to be available in the way that we should be.

Another problem is how to handle communities which are very divided. How can you be a bishop in such situations without falling between stools or sitting on the fence? I experienced division when I was an abbot. I decided that what unites people has to be very deep. It is the life of prayer. Get that right and much else falls into place.

*

Theodore was accompanied on his journey from Rome to Canterbury by the Abbot Adrian. Adrian had been asked by Pope Saint Vitalian to become Archbishop of Canterbury, but had recommended Theodore for that title. Apparently, he did not feel that his gifts and talents were those which would be needed to reorganise the Church in England. The fact that the pope accepted his recommendation of Theodore, and his own willingness to accompany Theodore to England, are clearly indications of a real strength of character and knowledge of self on the part of Adrian. He could so easily have accepted that position for himself, perhaps for reasons of political and personal prestige. Being asked by the pope to do this important work would suggest that he was thought capable of accomplishing it. After all, he had been an abbot in Naples where, we can assume, by the fact that the pope had wanted to appoint him to Canterbury, he had been an accomplished leader.

Since he had refused to become Archbishop of Canterbury, one would think that he could also have refused to accompany Theodore. Not only did he accompany Theodore to England, but while there became Theodore's constant companion and trusted adviser. To their mutual credit, England has reaped tremendous benefits from their recognition and acceptance of differing skills and talents.

Saint Paul's Monastery ruins, Jarrow

✝

CHAPTER SEVEN

BEṄEÐICT BISCOP

Saint Theodore of Tarsus and Saint Adrian journeyed to Canterbury from Rome with another person of considerable significance for the early Church of Anglo-Saxon England. This was Saint Benedict Biscop.

Benedict was born in Northumbria, of noble birth, and early in his life had been attached to the court of King Oswy. His service to Oswy must have been significant, because he was granted a large tract of land as well as numerous favours by the king. Rather than continuing and building a career in political and civil service, however, he chose to serve the Church.

His desire to do so led him on a pilgrimage to Rome to visit the tombs of Saints Peter and Paul. Returning to England, he began to show signs of a growing affection for the Church, for he expressed enthusiasm for certain Roman practices apparently unknown in England at the time. He made a second pilgrimage to Rome and, after some time there, went to the Isle of Lerins, off the southern coast of France, where he entered the monastery. He returned to Rome a third time, and it was then that he was asked to accompany Theodore of Tarsus and Adrian to England.

In England, Saint Benedict Biscop was appointed to some very important positions, including that of Abbot of the Monastery of Saints Peter and Paul at Canterbury. He is, however, remembered for the contribution he made by bringing to England books and sacred artifacts from his numerous trips to Rome. In so doing, he provided valuable sources for an expanding growth of knowledge and culture within our land.

There are three aspects, among many, of Benedict's contribution to English Christianity which merit special consideration. He returned from one of his trips to Rome with the Abbot John who was the arch-cantor of Saint Peter's. Abbot John came to England to teach Roman chant, an art form which had been revitalised and greatly advanced because of the reforms initiated by Pope Saint Gregory the Great who, we may recall, had first sent Augustine to England, and eventually to Canterbury.

The importance of Abbot John's contribution to English monastic life cannot be overestimated. At the very heart of the life of a monastery, and of its monks and nuns, is prayer and praise of God. Nine times a day, at certain appointed hours, the members of the monastery gather to pray. That prayer usually takes the form of chanting or singing what has come to be called 'The Divine Office'. Along with the Mass, The Divine Office is the official prayer of the Church. It is made up of a combination of psalms and readings from the scriptures, as well as readings from the writings of the saints and other sources which reflect the basic beliefs of Christianity and of the gospels. It is a practice of importance, for it has the added dimension of being universal in scope and reference, joining the prayer of a particular monastery or church, beyond its own local history and Christian practice, to the universal Church and to its richness of diversity and common life.

Saint Benedict Biscop's significant contribution to a universal perspective of Christianity for England was expressed in another way. At the mouth of the River Wear, he established the Monastery of Saint Peter. There he had a church built of stone in the Roman architectural style, bringing masons from France to fashion the stone. In this enterprise he also had the windows filled with glass, and thereby introduced a new art form to England. He also brought to England other French craftsmen to create sacred vessels, lamps and other artistic works. Benedict Biscop did not simply introduce a new style of art and architecture to English

Christianity, but set a tone for a new aesthetic sensibility for worship.

This is an important point, for in the worship of God nothing but the best is ever good enough. Beauty in architecture, music and decor is all part of giving honour to God. It enables us to raise minds and hearts up to God in prayer.

When I first came to Westminster Cathedral, there were people who wanted much more hymn singing from the congregation so they could feel that they were participating; they thought that listening to the choir was too much like being at a concert. I would respond to that by saying that you pray also with your ears and with your eyes. If the music and the singing are beautifully done, active participation is through what we see and what we hear. The trouble with contemporary liturgy, in my opinion, is that it is too verbal. People tend to think that you are only praying when you are talking, which is a mistake.

Beauty strikes the eye or the ear when the beauty of God is reflected. God speaks to us through beauty, and beauty is the correct language to use when we speak to God.

To return to Benedict Biscop, he established a second monastery, this one at Jarrow on the River Tyne. There, he amassed a great library of volumes from Rome and other parts of Europe, as well as from England. This prepared the way, and provided resources, for Saint Bede's incomparable history of Anglo-Saxon England, the primary source not only for this book, but also for any study of Anglo-Saxon England. It was at Jarrow, in 731, that Bede completed his *Ecclesiastical History of the English People*.

Saint Bede died in 735, having spent all his life in Jarrow. In fact, he left Jarrow only twice, once to pay a visit to York. He tells us that his great delight was in study, teaching and writing. We must never forget, however, that Bede was a man devoted to prayer as well as to education.

This period in English history was one of significant advance in culture and learning. Not only do we benefit today from Saint Benedict Biscop's contributions, but also from those of Saints Theodore of Tarsus and Adrian. The commitment and dedication of these three monk-bishops goes far beyond simply instilling the Roman tradition in England. Because of their own comprehensive knowledge of languages, Greek and Roman history and the arts, and Christian sources, they also contributed a real development in terms of our cultural and religious heritage. We might think of them as a second generation, building on the foundation established by Paulinus, Aidan and Hilda before them.

Grey Seals, Farne Islands

✠

ᴡɪʟꜰʀɪᴅ

Lest we think that the transition from a country divided by Celtic and Roman traditions to one under a unified Roman tradition was smooth and easy, we need only consider Saint Wilfrid. We saw him earlier at the Synod of Whitby where, at a very young age, he defended the Roman tradition. But we did not then consider how, as he argued for the primacy of Saint Peter and Rome, his exaggerated polemical style insulted the memory of Saint Columba and his followers so dear to the Celtic tradition. In response to that, Colman and some of his followers resigned from Lindisfarne and returned to Iona where the Celtic tradition continued to flourish for some time. This incident marks not only the beginning of Wilfrid's prominence as an ecclesiastical leader in Anglo-Saxon England, but also the beginning of the many difficulties created by his impulsive and explosive temperament.

He had entered the monastery at Lindisfarne, and while there began to question the Celtic tradition. In the year 653, with Benedict Biscop, he went on a journey to Rome to become further acquainted with practices of the Roman tradition. It was when he returned from this trip that he became abbot of the new Monastery of Ripon which Alfrid, King Oswy's son, had established. It was this office he held at the time of the Synod of Whitby.

Shortly afterwards, following the death of Colman's successor, Abbot Tuda, he became Abbot and Bishop of Lindisfarne. He went to Paris to be ordained bishop and remained there for some time. King Oswy, perhaps impatient at his prolonged absence and perhaps persuaded by Wilfrid's opponents, appointed Chad, who continued to adhere to the Celtic tradition, to Wilfrid's bishopric, though at York rather than Lindisfarne. Only after Saint Theodore of Tarsus exercised his authority as Archbishop of Canterbury, and after studying the situation, ruled in Wilfrid's favour, did Wilfrid become Bishop of York. He continued to encounter difficulties with kings and bishops throughout his lifetime.

Wilfrid opposed Theodore's creation of new dioceses in Northumbria, for the territories for these new dioceses were carved from Wilfrid's. Once again he went to Rome to keep his diocese and his authority. The pope recommended a compromise measure which allowed Wilfrid to maintain his authority in Northumbria and which also allowed Theodore to appoint other bishops to the area. As one would expect, Wilfrid did not get along with them. Nor was he welcomed back to Northumbria by the new King Alfrid who had him imprisoned.

It is worth noting that, amidst all these civil and ecclesiastical intrigues, Wilfrid's personal holiness and sincerity were never questioned. While in prison, he prayed constantly, singing psalms from memory.

It was not only Wilfrid's politics that led him into trouble. His detractors were also critical of his concerns for luxury, triumphalism, costly architectural projects, and his rich and flourishing monasteries. Even then, his personal sanctity and other good qualities drew many people towards him. Wilfrid was, indeed, a controversial figure, often contrasted with Aidan, a holy man living a very simple life.

Wilfrid is often presented as a flamboyant prelate who enjoyed the trappings of power and authority. However, it was Wilfrid, more than any other, who advanced the Roman tradition in England and envisaged a Church whose affiliation and perspective moved beyond the borders of the country towards the whole of the universal Church.

I am not certain that justice has been done to him. He was certainly a man of great zeal, believing profoundly in the importance of the monastic life. In that, he was clearly in the tradition of the Lindisfarne monks. It has to be remembered that Wilfrid had spent four years of his early life at Lindisfarne, and it would be quite wrong, I believe, to say that he was reacting against Lindisfarne when he promoted the Roman tradition and established his own foundations. He was rather like Benedict Biscop, who managed to marry in his person the best of both traditions.

His stormy, turbulent life ended in 709, and at the age of seventy-five he was buried in the cathedral he had built at Ripon. The story is told that, as his body was carried through the Abbey of Ripon, the monks heard the sound of birds and a rustling of wings which they thought to be choirs of angels leading Wilfrid into heaven. This story undoubtedly expresses their great esteem for his holiness.

Saint Cuthbert's Cell, Holy Island

✠

CHAPTER NINE

CUTHBERT

I suppose the idea of becoming a priest goes a long way back in my life. I was about the age of eleven when the thought first occurred to me. Then, after I had gone to Ampleforth as a schoolboy and came into contact with the monks there, I changed my mind and decided to join the community and become a monk. I always think that people join a religious order for one reason, and stay for the proper one. For instance, a person might join because he or she is attracted by that particular way of life. I know that I stayed because I became conscious that that was what God was calling me to do.

Whenever I am in Northumbria, I think about Cuthbert. He is, even today, a much-loved figure in the north, and I share with him a real love of the monastic life. Early in his youth he had entered the Monastery of Melrose, and, after being there for a while, became prior. He is fondly remembered for his visits to the neighbouring hamlets and cottages of the poor. He would gather the people around him, preaching, hearing confessions and doing whatever he could to alleviate their suffering.

He was asked to assume greater responsibilities and became Prior of Holy Island. I quite easily understand how, when he was at Holy Island, Cuthbert came to a crossroads in his life. He longed to be nearer to God, and his solution lay among the remote rocks, seven miles from Lindisfarne. Cuthbert became a hermit on Inner Farne, one of the Farne Islands.

A small cell and chapel were constructed for him on Inner Farne, where a spring supplied him with water and a small plot of land enabled him to grow barley for food. There he experienced peace and contentment in continual prayer and conversation with God.

One day, King Egfrid came from Bamburgh to Inner Farne, with a large retinue, to persuade Cuthbert to become Bishop of Lindisfarne. Although Cuthbert was most reluctant to accept their offer, in the end he did, and was a very successful bishop. We read that he was an immensely charming person and a good speaker. By combining his natural gifts with his great love of the scriptures and the Word of God, he was very effective. However, he had always been a reluctant bishop and never really enjoyed that role. After two years he resigned and returned to his cell on Inner Farne.

Cuthbert was already beginning to feel the effects of illness. He went to Inner Farne to be alone with God, and to spend the whole of his time with the light in his heart directed entirely on God. This is the life of the hermit.

Of course, people came to see him. Often the monks came over from Holy Island just to see how he was getting on or to consult him. However, Cuthbert had come to this very desolate place to pray. He even built high walls around his cell so that he would not be distracted by anything, even by the lovely things, the beauty, surrounding him. He wanted simply to let his eyes move up to the skies in heaven, as he himself said, because it was there that all his aspirations were directed.

Cuthbert's vocation was a special one, but not unique. Throughout the history of the Church there have always been those, men and women, who have wanted to give their whole, undivided attention to God. It is certainly a rare vocation and I believe that those who have it have been given a special gift.

When I was Abbot of Ampleforth, I had a monk who was refused permission for twenty years by my predecessor and myself to be a hermit. At the end of that time I let him do it, and he went up to the Yorkshire moors to be on his own and with God. I had been very undecided about whether to let him go ahead or not. It was a conversation with the Abbot General of the Cistercians which changed my mind. I told him the situation. I also said that I did not believe that monks of Ampleforth should become hermits. He told me quite simply that I was wrong!

A hermit is a man or woman who turns their back on society, not necessarily out of contempt for the world but because they want to give undivided attention to God. They are totally single-minded, living out the Lord's command to wait and watch. They are a powerful witness to the primacy of the spiritual in our lives. Saint Benedict seemed to have the idea that the perfection of the monastic life was the life of a hermit: there are certainly hints of that in his Rule.

In the year 687 Cuthbert died. At the moment of his death the monks who were with him lit torches to signal to the monks of Lindisfarne that this holy man had gone to God.

Durham Cathedral from the River Wear in winter

✠

the return of the saints

The great need of contemporary society is to rediscover the values of the gospel, particularly the centrality of the person of Jesus Christ who became man and enabled us to have a relationship with the Father. That is the basic Christian message to which all of the Northumbrian saints were giving witness. That was the message they were preaching.

What I admire so much in a person like Saint Aidan – as well as Saint Cuthbert and, indeed, Saint Wilfrid and Saint Hilda, the great abbess – is that these early English saints believed that Jesus revealed God to us, and also revealed the possibility of a relationship with God. They believed it with total conviction. Because they were people who made prayer the essential feature of their lives, it is clear, from studying their lives, that they had been touched by God in some way. There is no doubt in my mind that this combination of faith in the gospel and prayer in their lives transformed them, and led them to become such wonderful instruments of God's love.

Because of their own personal transformations into men and women of prayer, God could use them to bring the good news into the lives and hearts of the people to whom they preached. What I find so attractive is the simplicity of their message and the radical way in which they lived out their own Christian lives.

When I think of my own life as a bishop, my mind returns to these monks, Aidan and Cuthbert in particular. They remind me that, unless prayer is central in my life, then I cannot do my job as a bishop as efficiently and correctly as it should be done. I find that, as a bishop, I am constantly falling into the danger of feeling that, unless I am preoccupied with activity, seeing myself and others doing things, then I cannot be doing my job properly. It is a danger for all of us in the modern world. What I have learned from Aidan and Cuthbert is the importance of withdrawing from activity from time to time to be alone with God.

Every Lent Aidan went off to Inner Farne and lived the life of a hermit. Cuthbert did the same, even when he was a prior and a bishop. He would take time out to pray. Unless one can take time out to be alone with God, then one is not really thinking pastorally.

There is no passage in the scriptures that I personally find more moving and inspiring than the early sentences of Chapter 15 of Saint Luke's Gospel, where he tells the story of the shepherd leaving the ninety-nine to go in search of the one lost sheep. It is obviously irresponsible to leave ninety-nine sheep to wander off on their own, or to risk them doing so, to look for one that is lost!

Yet, as Christ was giving us the Word of God, we have to believe that God is that kind of person, one who will abandon no one. Once that is realised, it can make a great difference to people who feel alienated from the Church. They are not alienated. The Good Shepherd is looking for them and for those who are in any way troubled. We can be very consoled by the fact that God is seeking us all the time. For myself, if I did not think God was like that I do not know where I would be, or where any of us would be.

In every age there are stumbling blocks to receiving the gospel, but I still believe that there are people who are searching. They realise this when they are in crisis. You might lose a loved one through death. You might have a crisis in your business career. These are moments when you find yourself suddenly asking questions: Well, what is life all about? What are we

Durham Cathedral cloisters

here for? Where is it all leading? What happens after death? These are questions which haunt people in our day. The early Northumbrian monk-bishops brought answers to these questions, and those answers are as relevant today as they were in seventh- and eighth-century Northumbria.

There are other important questions in our day. People today have a great sense of compassion, of wanting to help those they see suffering. The world is increasingly becoming a global village and many people feel shock and horror when they see outrages and atrocities on their television screens. An appeal for a famine will always get an excellent response. There is a strong sense of justice, too, especially among young people.

These areas of spiritual search, of compassion and justice, are areas on which the Church can build. They are to do with the love of God and the love of neighbour. But they coexist in a culture which is largely opaque to the things of God. Unfortunately, many of the people who are searching and asking spiritual questions rarely go to church. For those who believe but do not go to church, I think we have to persuade them of the importance of doing so.

We need the support of others. We need to be part of a community. In my own life, saying the daily office all on my own is not the same as going to choir and joining with others. Communal prayer feeds individual prayer, individual prayer feeds communal prayer, and we need both. We also need to be involved with other people because we are social beings as well as individuals.

The values of the monastic life are timeless. They are values which are of fundamental importance in every age. I would list them in the following manner. I would say, first of all, that of timeless value is the centrality of the praise of God, something which is done very publicly, something done as a community through music, song and the recitation of the psalms. Second is the timeless value of the search for God, meditating on the Word of God, trying through prayer to discover God in the depths of one's heart and, of course, in one's world.

The centrality of praise of God and of rediscovering God in prayer are the key values of the monastic life, and they are no different from the values which, in fact, belong to every Christian. The monastic way is a particular way of living a Christian life, of doing it in a whole-hearted manner, as an important witness to the world. The monasteries throughout our land were great spiritual centres because they witnessed to the values of the gospel and to a conviction about the centrality of God and the Word of God.

The great tragedy in the history of our country was

the suppression of the monasteries, which resulted in the pillaging of their lands and the removal of lead from roofs and the stealing of stones to build nice country houses. But the desire for monastic life and for the centrality of God did not end with the dissolution of the monasteries. Young English men and women went abroad, became monks and nuns, returned to England when it was possible and refounded monasteries throughout the country. The monastic life goes on, and even in our day, monks and nuns have a role to play in the great drama of human life, exactly as Aidan and Hilda, Cuthbert and Wilfrid, Bede and Benedict had in their day.

Our culture still has residual effects of Christianity, but on the whole we live in a post-Christian society. We have to preach the gospel again. We have to re-evangelise our nation. I believe the monasteries have a very important role to play in that, not only as centres of spirituality, but also in the works in which they engage, particularly through the schools they administer.

When, as a child, I went with my family from Newcastle to Durham, I was always inspired by Durham Cathedral. It is a magnificent building. The foundation stone was laid in 1093, and I continue to be astonished by the realisation that the main part of the building was almost completed within forty years. Saint Bede's

Saint Bede's tomb, Galilee Chapel, Durham Cathedral

remains were brought here in 1370 and buried in the Galilee Chapel of the cathedral. There is something particularly fitting about Durham Cathedral being the place of Bede's tomb. When the cathedral was being built, and a monastic community was needed, monks from Jarrow accepted the invitation to establish a new community in 1093. There is, then, a continuity between Durham Cathedral and Jarrow Monastery, and between the place of Bede's burial and his life.

Down the ages, churches and cathedrals have been built to give honour and glory to God. Of course, the Church is not simply concerned with beautiful buildings and lovely ceremonials. It is also concerned with the good of the people, particularly their social welfare.

The saving of souls, as the expression goes, was a priority, but another priority was social welfare. The Church at the time of the Northumbrian saints, as the Church of today, became involved in social matters when it saw that the dignity of the human person had in some way been violated and diminished. That social dimension of the gospel also belongs to the monastic life and is a legacy we have received from the Northumbrian saints. Aidan did not hesitate to confront King Oswin when the latter rebuked him for giving his horse to a beggar. Nor did Hilda recoil from accepting Caedmon into Whitby. Wilfrid certainly did not sit back and ignore what he felt to be unjust practices. Cuthbert

Saint Cuthbert's tomb. Durham Cathedral

preached to the poor in the hamlets and villages surrounding Melrose.

I have learned from other people, and from bishops like Aidan and Cuthbert, that I, too, have to be a shepherd. I, too, have to be at the service of other people, especially those most in need. Aidan, in particular, was somebody who tried to bring the flock together as a shepherd should, giving them guidance, taking them to pastures where they might feed on the Word of God and on the sacraments.

In 1104, Durham Cathedral became Saint Cuthbert's final resting place. I say final because for over two hundred years his body had no resting place. The monks of Lindisfarne had to abandon their monastery in 875 because of the Viking raids and took Cuthbert's body with them.

I am always struck when I look at Cuthbert's tomb and its simple one-word inscription, 'Cuthbertus'. Its simplicity is moving because it is so consistent with his simplicity of life, and stands in contrast to the splendour of Durham Cathedral. It is right, of course, that we should build great cathedrals to the honour and glory of God. What is really important, however, is that we have the kinds of riches we associate with Cuthbert's holy life, and that is not easy for anyone.

Many people today are very confused. They have no purpose or meaning to their lives, but feel that they should have. When I meet people like that, I think of the story Venerable Bede tells of King Edwin's uncertainty. The sparrow's visit to the banqueting hall is short, like life itself. We do not know where the sparrow comes from or where it goes. For many of us, life is like that. We are confused. We do not know what it is all about, nor where we are going. As Saint Bede tells us, Edwin became Christian because this new religion could explain what happens before and after our short visit to the banqueting hall of life.

Religion is about truth, truth about God, truth about ourselves. It is the truth that makes us free. Saint Bede was a servant of truth. He dedicated his whole life to it. The saints about whom we have been thinking – Paulinus, Aidan, Hilda, Theodore of Tarsus, Benedict Biscop, Wilfrid, Cuthbert – were also apostles of truth, bringing knowledge of God to the people of their day. In so doing, they were building a society deeply influenced by Christian values.

We, in our day, face problems too. Our society is becoming ever more post-Christian. We no longer have shared moral values. There is much confusion about the purpose of life. But we can be inspired by the saints of Anglo-Saxon England, and do in our day what they did in theirs. Perhaps we, too, might create a new Golden Age for Christianity.

Basil Hume walking on a Northumbrian beach

EPILOGUE

✝

The saints of Northumbria still live on in the north.
I remember looking for the site where Edwin had
his camp, near where Paulinus baptised. I remember
walking up the hill and meeting a child of about eight.
I asked her where the camp was and she pointed it out
to me, and I asked her if she knew what happened
there and she did. I asked if she had heard of so and
so, and she said she had. I said, 'How do you know?'
and she said they learnt it at school. I was very
impressed. Saint Cuthbert is still alive in the north.